A Drive into the Gap

A Field Notes Brand Book
July 2012

All rights reserved.
Copyright ©2012 by Kevin Guilfoile

Cover and book design
Copyright ©2012 Field Notes Brand

No part of this book may be reproduced or transmitted in any form
or by any means, electronic or mechanical, including but not limited
to photocopying, recording, or by any information storage and
retrieval system, without permission in writing from the publisher.

ISBN 978-0-9858316-0-8

Field Notes Brand Books
c/o Coudal Partners, Inc., 400 North May Street,
Chicago, Ill 60642

Printed in the United States of America

10 9 8 7 6 5 4 3 2 1

A Drive into the Gap

Kevin Guilfoile

FIELD NOTES BRAND BOOKS

Portland, Ore. • *Chicago, Ill.*

"Memory takes a lot of poetic license.
It omits some details; others are exaggerated,
according to the emotional value of the articles it touches,
for memory is seated predominantly in the heart."

—*Tennessee Williams*, The Glass Menagerie

ONE

My first memory is of my father carrying a hammer into our bedrooms and smashing open our piggy banks on the night Roberto died.

I couldn't have known what was happening. I didn't know about the sputtering airplane, carrying one Major League superstar and too many supplies for earthquake victims in Nicaragua. But I might have understood what Roberto meant to my dad.

Three years earlier, as my father arrived for his first day on the job with the Pittsburgh Pirates, he had been intercepted by Dick Stockton in the parking lot of McKechnie Field, the Bucs' spring training home in Bradenton, Florida. Stockton is a first-tier play-by-play announcer now, but in 1970 he was a Pittsburgh television sports anchor, and he asked if Dad was the team's new public relations director. When my father said he was, Stockton said he would like an interview with Roberto Clemente. My father explained he'd only been on the job a few minutes, and that he hadn't even met Clemente yet. Nevertheless, he would see what he could do.

My dad has Alzheimer's now so I can't ask him what happened next, but when his memories were still

A DRIVE INTO THE GAP

present he took out a yellow legal pad and wrote down many of his baseball stories. In these pages he describes his first encounter with Roberto. Dad introduced himself as the new PR guy, and in the next breath asked if Clemente would do an interview with the sports director from KDKA-TV.

> *Roberto reacted with a three or four minute outburst, combining English and Spanish, to let me know exactly how he felt about Stockton. Apparently he and Dick had had a falling-out some time ago over something Stockton had said on the air.*
>
> *Then Roberto paused, regained his composure, and looked at me with a little smile. "Would it help you if I did the interview?" he asked.*
>
> *"Well, it's my first day on the job and I'm trying to get off on the right foot," I said. "Yes, it would help me if you would talk to him."*
>
> *Clemente nodded and said, "Ok. For you I will do it, my friend." He finished dressing, walked out on the field, and gave an interview to Dick Stockton for the first time in years.*

That night in my bedroom, early in the morning on New Year's Day, 1973, I don't think my dad had words for what he was feeling. He'd just finished a call with Joe Brown, the Pirates' general manager. In his grief, Joe didn't hang up the phone on his end, which, in the context of early seventies telecommunications, meant our home phone was disconnected. So Dad poured change from his kids' banks into an old sock that he would carry, along with his little green address book, a mile through the cold and snow to a parking lot pay phone outside a general store, and from there he would tell the world that his friend Roberto was dead.

TWO

From the notes of Bill Guilfoile:

In the 1960s, during my years with the New York Yankees, I shared an office with Jackie Farrell, the diminutive, wizened, Yankee good-will ambassador. He was loved by everyone who knew him, and hardly a day went by when he wasn't out, either on a speaking engagement or attending some other function.

The first week I was with the club, Jackie told me a story, which, at one time or another, I'm sure he shared with every Yankee employee. It seems years ago Jackie was a wrestling promoter living in Hoboken, New Jersey. One evening his neighbor stopped by for a cup of coffee and during the conversation he asked if Jackie would be interested in arranging some local gigs for his teen-age son, Frankie, whom the father felt might have a future as a singer. Jackie turned him down, saying, "If he were a wrestler I might be interested, but singers are a dime-a-dozen." Over the years Jackie often wondered how his life might have been different if

A DRIVE INTO THE GAP

he had seized the opportunity so many years ago to become Frank Sinatra's manager.

One day a news item appeared in the New York papers announcing that a scene from the movie "The Detective" starring Frank Sinatra and Lee Remick would be filmed at Yankee Stadium.

In no time our office was overrun with Yankee secretaries, pleading with Jackie to introduce them to Sinatra when he arrived for the filming. Jackie assured everyone that he'd be delighted to oblige, but as the day approached he became very nervous. "I haven't seen any of the Sinatras in twenty years," he confessed to me. "Frankie will never recognize me, everyone will think I'm a liar, and it's going to be the most embarrassing day of my life."

The day before the scheduled filming he told me that he planned to take a sick day. But he showed up in the morning looking pale as a ghost.

As word trickled down that the crews were arriving, that cameras were being set up, that Lee Remick's hairdresser was on site, that limousines were arriving—the excitement and tension in our little room mounted.

The women in the office began tugging at Jackie to take them out for the promised introduction. Finally, like the Pied Piper of Hamelin, a reluctant Jackie Farrell led the entourage up the stairs, through the stadium lobby, up the ramp, and out into the stands.

It was a cloudy, damp, and foggy morning. The cameras were focused in the vicinity of the Yankee dugout, and there was Sinatra, in trench coat and fedora, preparing for the shoot.

The women began shoving Jackie down the aisle, and he finally called out in a weak voice, "Hey.

Frankie." There was no reaction and the group surged anxiously forward. He tried again, only a little bit louder. "Hey. Frankie." Still no response. More pushing.

Now, about thirty feet away, Jackie gave it his best effort. "Hey. Frankie." Sinatra turned, peered through the drizzle, and yelled "My god, it's Jackie Farrell!" He ran up the steps, lifted Jackie off his feet, and gave him a big hug, as tears streamed down Jackie's face.

THREE

"Time is the thing that keeps everything from happening all at once."

I think the first person who said that was the French philosopher and Nobelist Henri Bergson, although I've also seen it attributed to *The Sisterhood of the Traveling Pants*. Whoever, it's the principle that I use to understand what has happened to my father since the caulk of Alzheimer's has filled in the synapses of his brain.

To my dad, I am five years old and also a novelist. I am forty-three years old and also an undergrad at the University of Notre Dame. I am an assistant media relations director for the Houston Astros and I am not yet old enough to drive. I am a Little League coach in La Grange, Illinois, and a Little League player in Bethel Park, Pennsylvania. I also work in advertising.

My mother knows me as all these things, too, but she understands time as an organizing principle, that I was each of these things at a different stage of my life. My father does not. To him I am all of these things at once. He lives in an unrelenting present, with no real concept of yesterday or tomorrow.

My mother is easier for him to recognize, because she has always been the same, reliable thing to him. But he does sometimes offer to carry her books to class.

His personality is present, if his memories are a jumble. He is still funny, and surprisingly quick with one-liners to crack up the staff at the facility where he lives. He is exceedingly polite, same as he ever was. He is good at faking a casual conversation, especially on the phone. But if you sit and talk with him for a long time, he gets very anxious. He starts tapping his forehead with his fingers. "Shouldn't we be going?" he'll say. You tell him there's no place we need to be, but thirty seconds later he'll ask again, "Shouldn't we be going?" He doesn't mean he needs to be somewhere else in ten minutes, he means that he needs to be somewhere else now. He needs to be *everywhere now*. My father's mind bombards him constantly with logical and logistical impossibilities.

What happens to memories when they're collapsed inside time like this? They don't exactly disappear, they just become impossible to unpack. And so my father, who loved stories so much—who loved to tell them, who loved to hear them—can no longer comprehend them. The structure of any story, after all, is that this happened and then that happened and he can't make sense of any sequence. He doesn't read anymore, although I've caught him more than once staring at the pages of one of my books. I ask him if he's watching any baseball this season and he always says, "Every chance I get!" But he doesn't really watch TV, and I know he couldn't follow a baseball game anyway, with its repeating three-act structures (starter, reliever, closer; lead-off, clean-up, bottom of the order) and every inning like a new chapter, with its own climaxes and cliffhangers.

A DRIVE INTO THE GAP

He likes to talk about the weather. The weather is right now. It's sunny. It's cloudy. It's snowing. It's raining. That is something he can process and understand.

His own life, his life in baseball, is present but vague. Ask him about Mickey Mantle, whom he befriended and worked with for ten years, and he'll smile and say, "Boy! What a player!" But ask him about the night he watched Mantle virtually crawl from the empty Yankee Stadium clubhouse because Mantle was in such pain after each game he could hardly walk, that story is just out of reach.

That is the real hell of this disease. His own identity has become a puzzle he can't solve.

Objects have stories, too. Puzzles that need to be solved. Like a pair of baseball bats, for instance, that each passed through Roberto Clemente's hands before they passed through my father's. One hung on my bedroom wall throughout my childhood. The other is in the Baseball Hall of Fame.

These objects never forget, but they never tell their stories either.

Without a little bit of luck, we'd never hear them.

FOUR

I didn't really have a life *in baseball*, the way my dad did. I had a life *around* baseball. In *proximity* to baseball. And it was pretty great.

From the time I was a baby and my dad was working for the New York Yankees, until I was in the fifth grade, when Dad left the Pirates to become Vice President of the Baseball Hall of Fame, I probably went to forty or fifty Major League baseball games a year. Maybe more. In Pittsburgh, I camped at Three Rivers Stadium, sitting with my mom and brothers and sister four rows behind first base. After the game we would wait hours for my dad in his office. I would read, or play with his typewriter, pounding out the opening paragraphs to science-fiction stories I would never finish. The Pirates' offices at Three Rivers were cool and windowless and smelled like cigars. I've never smoked, but to this day I love second-hand cigar smoke, which I associate with summer and baseball the way the old song does peanuts and Cracker Jack.

Every time we'd enter the lobby, I'd linger by the 1971 World Series trophy, counting its golden pennants. I met Bing Crosby in that lobby, and the guy who played Squiggy on *Laverne & Shirley*.

A DRIVE INTO THE GAP

When we moved to Cooperstown, hours from even a small city, we didn't go to games nearly as much. But there in the country we had our own ballpark: Doubleday Field, the apocryphal birthplace of baseball. I played all my high school games—and all my American Legion and PONY League games, as well—not on some knobby school field surrounded by aluminum bleachers and chain link, but in full view of tourist spectators on the pristine infield of an historic, 10,000-seat ballpark.

Throughout the summer the best youth baseball teams from around the East would bus to Cooperstown to play on Doubleday Field. The team they would play there was usually ours. We often played two, sometimes three games a day.

Most of our players had summer jobs so we would sub in and out as best we could. I was the stock boy at the Farm and Home Bargain Center directly across the street from the ballpark. I'd wear my uniform to work, stock the shelves, vacuum the store, then grab my mitt and run across the street. I'd play a few innings until word came that a truck had arrived full of Cabbage Patch dolls or kerosene or whatever, and I'd dash across Main Street to unload it, just as another kid, still smelling of chores from his family farm, pulled up to take my place.

We were rarely in the same league as the teams we were playing—they were often state champion all-star squads from much bigger towns. We lost a lot. I used to call us youth baseball's Washington Generals, after the basketball team that barnstorms the country getting clobbered night after night by the Harlem Globetrotters, except in our case the good teams would ride a bus all night for the privilege of playing us on our home field. Winning stopped being the point for us. It was about *playing*, playing as much as you could every day that you could.

If I had been smart I would have saved a lineup card from each of those games. Who knows how many one-day Major Leaguers we played against as kids.

But it wasn't the future heroes of baseball that defined summers in Cooperstown as much as the ones that had already made history. I met almost every living baseball great. I talked hitting with Ted Williams and base running with Cool Papa Bell. I stayed away from my parents' house so Ken Burns's crew could film interviews for his baseball documentary unmolested in the living room. I sat at my own dining room table with former baseball commissioner Bowie Kuhn as legendary Yankees pitcher Waite Hoyt spun first-hand yarns about Babe Ruth.

Years before we lived there, Joe DiMaggio and Marilyn Monroe not only ate dinner at that same table with a previous owner, but helped with the dishes afterward. Marilyn Monroe doing dishes at the same sink where I washed dishes every night. That's a mental picture that will make a thirteen-year-old kid's head explode.

A few years after Roberto died, his widow Vera and their three sons came to our house in the Pittsburgh suburbs for dinner. My parents told us not to tell anyone, but I was seven years old, so I told everybody. The grown-ups shooed us outside so they could talk, and while my siblings and I played Wiffle ball with Roberto, Jr., Enrique, and Luis, there was a neighborhood kid hiding in every bush and tree. Until Enrique waved them all in to play with us.

We played and laughed until it was dark. No one even took a photograph.

In 1978, my older brother Tom served as the Pirates' batboy. You can see Tom sitting, crosslegged, front row center, on the Topps 1979 Pirates team baseball card

A DRIVE INTO THE GAP

(the photo having been taken a season earlier). Every time Tom is near a sports memorabilia shop he goes in and buys all the '79 Pirates team cards. I don't know how many he's hoarded, hundreds probably, in a futile attempt to drive up the price. You can still get one for a nickel.

One day, a few hours before a game with Philadelphia, Pirates player John Milner asked Tom to get him coffee. The pot in the Pirates' clubhouse was empty, so Tom ran over to the visiting clubhouse. As he was pouring a cup someone shouted at him, "What the hell are you doing here?"

When Tom turned, Phillies shortstop Larry Bowa was off his stool and getting right in his face. Tom was in a Pirates uniform, but he was barely a teenager. At 5'10", Bowa would have towered over him. When Tom explained that he was just getting coffee for Milner, Bowa launched a barrage of expletives and spittle. He told my brother to put down the cup, and said that Tom should tell John Milner to go to hell, too.

Tom went back to the Pirates' dugout and explained to Milner why he couldn't get his coffee, and then returned to his pregame chores—organizing equipment, running errands, polishing shoes and helmets. He watched from a distance as Milner walked over to the batting cage and said something to Pirates captain Willie Stargell.

The game started. John Candelaria was pitching for the Pirates. And as Larry Bowa walked up to bat in the first inning, Milner sat down on the bench next to my brother. Candelaria fired and his first pitch was a fastball at Bowa's head that knocked him down in a cloud of dirt. As Bowa got to his feet, brushing clay from his uniform, my brother could see Stargell yelling something at him from first base.

In the dugout, Milner told my brother, "That was for you."

On the short list of truly epic things that can happen to a fourteen-year-old boy in summer, a future Hall of Famer ordering an All-Star pitcher to knock down an All-Star shortstop in the middle of a Major League pennant race because the shortstop was a jerk to you blows them all away.

Except maybe Marilyn Monroe washing dishes at your sink.

FIVE

Jerry Reuss was a great practical joker and one of his classic stunts occurred in the '80s, after he was traded from the Pirates to the Los Angeles Dodgers.

Prior to a game in which Tom Niedenfuer was the Dodgers' starting pitcher and Frank Pulli was the home plate umpire, Reuss removed one of the game balls from the ball bag and autographed it as follows: "Frank—Hope you're enjoying the game, Tommy Lasorda."

Niedenfuer noticed the writing on the ball, but he pitched it anyway and the batter fouled the pitch into the stands. After the game, Niedenfuer told Lasorda he thought it was pretty funny that the manager was writing messages to the umpires on the game balls. Lasorda didn't have any idea what he was talking about.

When he arrived home, Lasorda's wife asked Tommy about the autographed ball, as well. Now Tommy was really puzzled. Jo explained to him that a fan sitting in front of her had caught a foul ball and was amazed to find it already signed by the Dodgers' manager.

Not only that, said the fan, who introduced himself as Frank, Lasorda had somehow inscribed it to him.

SIX

My dad loved stories. He loved that Jackie Farrell and Frank Sinatra story because it's a story about stories. About the fear that no one will believe your story. It's also about the ways grace and redemption can result from a simple act of kindness. My father believed that was true with all his heart.

He also loved practical jokes. He loved telling stories about great practical jokes.

Tony Bartirome was the Pirates' trainer throughout the 1970s. Whenever there was a rookie in the clubhouse, the Pirates' players would take him aside and point at Tony, who was only about 5'9", and say, "You know Tony can deadlift three guys off the floor at one time." The rookie would say, "No way," and the players would say, "Pound for pound, Tony Bartirome is the strongest man in baseball." Eventually the new kid would demand some feat of strength as proof. After a lot of begging, sometimes over several days, Tony would reluctantly agree. He'd tell the rookie to pick out the two biggest guys in the clubhouse. Then he'd tell him to lie on the floor and the other two players would lock arms with the kid on either side. Tony would stretch and take

A DRIVE INTO THE GAP

some breaths. He'd rip a phone book in half. He would lean over the three men on the carpet.

And then the rest of the team would cover the helpless rookie in shaving cream.

Worked every time. My dad was always sure he was in the clubhouse to see it.

When he was at the Hall of Fame, a co-worker's wife came to my dad's office with a tasteful oil landscape of some wooded scene from upstate New York. She had bought it for her husband's birthday and since my dad was often first to arrive at the Museum, she wondered if he would mind sneaking into her husband's office the morning of his birthday and hanging it on the wall before he arrived. *Of course*, my dad said. *I'd be happy to*.

Then he went down into the Hall storage room and found the most atrocious amateur painting he could find. I can't remember who the subject was—Oscar Gamble or Mookie Wilson or maybe Mark "The Bird" Fidrych—but it was done in a poor imitation of LeRoy Neiman. It was grotesque and enormous, taking up almost a whole wall.

And every day for weeks, until she came in one day to meet him for lunch, this fellow had to go home and tell his wife how much he loved the painting she had given him as a present.

Some of Dad's stories were plainly false. He used to tell us about a turtle he and his brother found when they were kids. It had obviously been somebody's pet as it had the word "POPEYE" printed across its shell. They kept it for several weeks but eventually their parents convinced them that they had to let it go. They took him into the woods, to a cool spot near a stream, and set him on the ground. Popeye took about ten slow steps, then he turned around, stood on his hind legs, and waved goodbye.

My entire life, my father has always insisted that story is true.

My dad's brother recently sent me a series of letters he wrote to my father as Dad's dementia was approaching a point of no return. In them he relates stories from their childhood in Fond du Lac, Wisconsin, hoping one of them might stimulate some old memory.

One of his stories was about a woman on their street named Mrs. Pinther. My uncle wrote:

> *The most notable memory there is that she had a boarder in the basement named Hans. He spoke with a German accent and we were convinced he was a Nazi spy. One day Hans was no longer around and we figured the FBI had picked him up.*

My father told us that story many times when we were kids. Except in my father's version their street had been filled with black sedans and serious men with pistols bulging under their blazers. Hans was led out of Mrs. Pinther's basement in handcuffs, shouting his allegiance to the Führer as my dad and his brother peered out their bedroom window through the narrow slit between closed drapes. Hans had been caught spying at the Mercury Marine factory in town. The war had come home to Fond du Lac.

That story was so much better.

SEVEN

On Saturday, September 30, 1972, Roberto Clemente arrived at Three Rivers Stadium tired and frustrated. He had 2,999 hits for his career, and the night before he would have become only the eleventh player in baseball history with 3,000 hits except the official scorer had changed one of his at-bats from an infield hit to an error. Roberto hadn't slept at all, but he desperately wanted to get to 3,000. It had been a long season. He was getting older. He needed to take a couple games off before the playoffs, but he wanted the 3,000-hit gorilla off his back first.

He struck out in the first inning, but in the fourth he knocked it solid for a double. No scorekeeper could take this one away. On the radio, legendary Pirates broadcaster Bob Prince was calling it: "Bobby hits a drive into the gap in left-center field! There she is!"

The game was stopped briefly. Clemente acknowledged the crowd. Second-base umpire Doug Harvey retrieved the ball and handed it to Roberto, who chucked it to first-base coach Don Leppert.

Roberto would score moments later on a Manny Sanguillen single and in the following inning he came out of the lineup.

After the game, my dad went down to the clubhouse and waded through a media scrum to Clemente's locker. Sportswriters were asking Roberto how he chose the bat that got him his 3,000th hit. Roberto told the *New York Times* that Willie Stargell helped him pick out the bat. "I haven't been swinging good lately so Willie picked out one of my bats... a heavier one that I have been using," Roberto is quoted as saying. "He handed it to me and told me to 'go get it.'"

He told Bob Smizik of the *Pittsburgh Press* a slightly different story. According to Smizik:

> *Clemente was undecided whether to use one of his own bats or a Richie Hebner model in his second turn at the plate. "I decided I better use my own," he said. "If I was going to get the hit I wanted to do it with my own bat."*

Hebner was the Pirates' third baseman in 1972, but forty years later he doesn't remember Roberto saying anything to him during the game about borrowing his bat. What Hebner remembers most about that day is the crowd. "There were only about 13,000 people there. It was a Saturday, and Pittsburgh's a big football town, but that was just unbelievable to me."

It's hard to imagine it today. The Pirates were the defending world champions. They had clinched the division title and were headed for the playoffs. One of the biggest stars in a century of Pittsburgh baseball was about to do something that only ten players in the game had ever done. And Three Rivers Stadium was four-fifths empty. I wonder how many Pittsburghers today claim they were there to watch Clemente get number 3,000 when in reality they had chosen to watch an 0-3 Pitt football team lose to Northwestern instead.

A DRIVE INTO THE GAP

When my dad got to his locker, he asked Roberto for the bat he used to get number 3,000. Clemente handed it over—a Louisville Slugger model U1 with a "21" scribbled on the flared knob in felt pen—and my father packed it up and sent it to the Baseball Hall of Fame in Cooperstown.

Three months later, almost to the day, Clemente would be dead. A plane he chartered to carry humanitarian supplies to earthquake-ravaged Nicaragua would crash after takeoff. Number 3,000 would be the last regular-season hit of his career.

Seven years later Dad would take a job with the Hall of Fame, eventually becoming its Vice President. For most of his time there that bat, one of the most popular artifacts in the museum, was in a display case just outside his office. He would have seen it every single day.

No piece of memorabilia in the entire building had a more meaningful, more personal connection to my father than the bat Roberto Clemente used to collect his 3,000th hit.

EIGHT

One afternoon during our stay in Puerto Rico, Roberto and his wife Vera drove us around San Juan, showing us the city they were so proud of. During the day we walked the streets and stopped twice to eat. Although Roberto was universally recognized, not once was he approached for an autograph. The next day I mentioned this to a Puerto Rican newspaperman. "Oh," he said. "No one would ever think of asking him for an autograph when he was with friends. We respect him too much." I thought this was an interesting contrast to what athletes experience in the States."

NINE

I only worked in baseball for three seasons so, unlike my dad, I never forged any lasting friendships with professional ballplayers.

But I was on the job only a few hours before I made an enemy of one.

I was a twenty-year-old American studies major making $500 a month as an intern in the Pirates' media relations department. Barry Bonds was a twenty-four-year-old leadoff hitter, a player with huge potential, but he wasn't yet the superstar he would be a few years later, or the muscle-bound superman he would become a few years after that. The season I spent with Barry he had a respectable nineteen home runs and an impressive thirty-two stolen bases, but he batted just .248. Four members of the Pirates' starting lineup—Bobby Bonilla, Gary Redus, Jay Bell, and R.J. Reynolds—each hit for a better average on a fifth-place team. No one was calling Barry Bonds a future Hall of Famer yet.

On a typical day at Three Rivers Stadium I did research and helped with media inquiries and wrote articles for various in-house publications. During games I worked in the press box, basically as a gofer. When the team was home I had one other chore, which I should have been able to do in about fifteen minutes. Because of Barry Bonds it often took more than two hours.

Every morning I would get a list of names from the Community Relations department—sick kids in hospitals, mostly, or other charity and management requests—and I would walk down to the clubhouse with a folder of glossy photos to get autographs. I tried to limit the number of signatures per player—I don't think there was ever a day when I brought more than four or five requests for any one person.

Now that I'm a novelist who is often asked to sign his name in books, it seems absurd that I was once worried about burdening anyone with the task of signing autographs. I think I can speak for almost every writer I know when I say it's a privilege to sign books for readers. The idea that I'd ever feel put out by someone asking for my autograph seems ridiculous.

Nevertheless, if celebrity is currency in America, writer fame surely has the lowest street value. No matter how many books a novelist sells, no one is going to ask him to appear on *Dancing with the Stars*. Outside of book events and his own neighborhood hardly any writer (except maybe the memorably featured Stephen King) ever gets recognized. Robert B. Parker, who wrote something like fifty novels and who was one of the most popular authors on the planet, was once spotted by a fan while dining at a restaurant in his own hometown of Boston and he was so pleasantly surprised he wrote an essay about it for the *New York Times*.

That's how rarely it happens.

I can't imagine what it must be like to be movie-actor famous. Or athlete famous. To never be able to finish a meal at a restaurant or shop for pants or go to a movie without being interrupted by a stranger. And

A DRIVE INTO THE GAP

while every reader I've ever met has been gracious, for the truly famous, obsessed signature-seekers in malls and movie theaters aren't always so deferential. I have seen a lot of bad behavior from fans that think an out-of-uniform athlete owes them his attention, without regard for the hundreds of others who make the same demand of him every day.

A few years later when I was working for the Astros, Houston reliever Xavier Hernandez was walking back to the spring training clubhouse in Kissimmee, Florida. He was stopped by a fan and pretty soon there was a line of kids and adults who wanted his autograph. Xavier no doubt had places to be, and family waiting for him, but he stopped and signed photos and balls and programs. Finally the last kid in line, probably eight or nine years old, took his scorecard after Xavier had signed it and said, "Thank you, Mr. Hernandez." Xavier called him back. "Do you know I've been signing autographs for half an hour and you were the *only* person who said thanks?" Hernandez picked his glove off the ground where he'd dropped it, autographed it down the thumb, and handed it to the kid.

For athletes, locker rooms are sanctuaries. They might have to deal with reporters on occasion, but the rest of the time the clubhouse is a place where they can relax and eat and watch television and read fan mail and decompress and joke around and cuss and not have to worry about crowds of fans monopolizing their time and never saying thank you. So I was sensitive to all that and most of the ballplayers treated me with kindness, or at least respect. A few probably even hoped their name would be on one of my Post-its—the fact that some kid had asked for their autograph being a good sign for their careers. Others thought of me as a minor nuisance that could be disposed of with a few seconds of effortless Sharpie wielding.

And then there was Barry Bonds.

Barry wasn't the kind of jerk who was nice to people only when he needed something from them. As far as I could tell, Barry was pretty much an ass to everybody all the time. I remember one game when Barry hit a home run that set some obscure record and the twelve-year-old boy who caught the ball returned it to the clubhouse so Barry could have it. The next day I asked him to sign a different ball to send to the kid as a thank-you. Barry signed it (after about twenty minutes of pretending he couldn't hear me), but when I asked him to write *To Christopher* on it, or maybe *Thanks Christopher*, Barry refused. "I signed it and he'll like it," he told me. "He'll take whatever I give him."

Most of the players had as little to do with Barry as possible. Bobby Bonilla had a locker next to his. At the time Bonilla was a bigger star than Bonds and he was one of the few players in that clubhouse who was on friendly terms with Barry. Instead of berating me directly or just ignoring me, Barry would sometimes talk about me like I wasn't there. Sometimes he would tell Bobby that I was lying to them and these autographs weren't for fans and that I was just selling these pictures to professional dealers, that I was another no-talent white man exploiting black men who possessed real ability. Sometimes he would tell Bobby that the two of them were like slaves and I was... actually, I never understood who I was supposed to be in Barry's slavery scenario. Anyway, when Barry was around, Bobby would shake his head and tell me to go away, and then when Barry would leave the room Bobby would wave me back and apologize and sign everything I had for him.

Eventually I figured out a system, but it required patience and timing. There was only one person in that clubhouse whose opinion mattered to Barry Bonds, and

A DRIVE INTO THE GAP

that was the manager, Jim Leyland. I soon realized Barry would never allow Leyland to see him being disrespectful to me. So I would get signatures from the other players, and then I would wait for Leyland to come out of his office—which some days he never did. But if Leyland did walk by, I would be standing next to Barry with a Sharpie and he would scowl and give me what I needed. Until the next day.

One homestand I was getting a lot of pressure to get Barry's signature on a ball, and he wasn't having anything to do with me. Every couple of hours I'd get a phone call asking where it was and I'd go down to the clubhouse and stalk Barry and he'd tell me to piss off or turn his back and leave when he saw me. I got so frustrated I grabbed a couple of balls from somewhere and hid myself away in a conference room and practiced his signature until it was passable.

I never tried to pass those autographs as Barry's—I was just blowing off steam—but there had been a day when it was common to do so. In the 1960s, Clemente's heyday, most teams would have had a couple folks in the front office or the clubhouse—my dad was one of them for the Yankees—who were experts at forging the signatures of their top players. Dad used to joke that there were probably as many Mickey Mantle balls signed by Bill Guilfoile as there were balls signed by Mickey Mantle.

The prevailing attitude among ball clubs and players back then was that balls and bats and signatures were things that could make people happy. They weren't appreciating investments with certificates of authenticity the way they are today. Most adults would have been too embarrassed to even ask for one. So if a committee of Yankees employees could produce three times the number of Mantle autographs, that would just make three times as many kids happy.

No ball club would ever do that anymore. If you mail a Derek Jeter baseball card to the New York Yankees today, you'll probably get it returned untouched, with a bumper sticker, a pocket schedule, and a boilerplate apology.

TEN

I call people from my dad's life to verify some of his old stories. Every single one of them says the same thing after I introduce myself. They even use almost identical words.

Everyone loved your dad.

ELEVEN

My father has lots of old baseball bats given to him by players he worked with over the years. He has Mantle bats from his years with the Yankees, and Willie Stargell and Dave Parker bats from his days with the Pirates. The one I always loved best was an Adirondack model. This Adirondack was peculiar because instead of a signature burned into the barrel, it just had the name embossed in modest block letters: R CLEMENTE. On the bottom of the knob Roberto had written a tiny "37" in ballpoint pen, presumably to indicate its weight: thirty-seven ounces. It also had a series of scrapes around the middle where someone had scratched off the trademark stripe that wrapped around all Adirondack bats. Former Pirates general manager Joe Brown gave my dad this bat several years after Roberto died. For much of my childhood it hung on the wall of my bedroom, on a long rack with about a dozen other game-used bats.

In 1993, the same summer I left the Astros and started as a creative director for Coudal Partners in Chicago, my dad had been working at the Hall of Fame for more than a decade. His old friend Tony Bartirome, the one-time Pirates trainer and feats-of-strength prankster, came

A DRIVE INTO THE GAP

to Cooperstown for a visit. Tony and his wife went to dinner with my folks and then came back to our house on Lake Street to chat. The only way to go to the first-floor washroom in that house was through my old bedroom and, on a trip there, Tony noticed that Adirondack of Clemente's hanging on the wall.

Tony carried it into the living room. He said to Dad, "Where did you get this bat?" My dad told him that Joe Brown had given him the bat as a gift, sometime in the late seventies. "Bill," Tony said. "This is the bat Roberto used to get his 3,000th hit."

My father was confused by this. "That's impossible," he told Tony. "The day he hit 3,000 I went down to the clubhouse and Roberto himself handed me the bat he used. I sent it to the Hall of Fame. I walk by it every day."

"Well," Tony said. "I have a story to tell you."

And when he was done, my dad's head must have been on a teacup ride.

Actually, I'm pretty sure he thought Tony was putting him on. Both Tony and my dad had long histories as practical jokers, and the jokes my dad liked best were the long cons, where you can convince someone of a story that alters their reality in some small way. It was best if you never admitted what you did.

From that perspective, this story would have been a *doozy*, as Dad was fond of saying. As the person who acquired the bat from Roberto the day he got the hit, my father provided the provenance of the bat, certifying that it was the real thing. As Vice President of the Baseball Hall of Fame, he was now one of its guardians. If it turned out to be true that my father had the real bat in his home all along, this would be a major scandal in the memorabilia world. Many people, especially those who didn't know my dad, would assume he had made the switch himself. My father's reputation for fairness and honesty, established over more than three decades in baseball, would be tarnished forever.

So Dad tried to call Tony's bluff.

He got out his typewriter and worked up a statement for Tony to sign.

> *This Adirondack, Roberto Clemente model, is the bat he used to achieve his 3,000th hit in 1972. He had a preference for this Adirondack bat, but since he was under contract with Louisville Slugger, he asked me to scrape off the black ring on the bat handle, which is the identifying characteristic of the Adirondack bat. I did so with a scalpel and he used this bat for his 3,000th (and final) hit.*
>
> *Tony Bartirome*
> *August 13, 1993*

He signed it. Tony was absolutely certain of his story.

The next day my dad took that statement into work and informed other officials at the Hall of Fame. Dad never told me exactly what they did next, but I know they looked into it and apparently decided that the story couldn't be true.

No doubt this was a relief to my father. But I know he loved the story. He told it to me several times. He always said, "Wouldn't it be something if that were true?" and he would chuckle. It was a great baseball story. If he hadn't been a character in the tale, he'd have wanted it to be real.

But it turns out my dad didn't know the whole story behind that Clemente bat in my old bedroom. Turns out Tony Bartirome didn't know it either. It's a story about memory. It's a story about chance. It's a story about stories. It's a story about the very nature of sports and memorabilia.

TWELVE

The problem with history is that every story has multiple witnesses, but no witness ever has the entire truth. This happens to be what both of my first two novels are about. And the next one, too.

A few years ago I considered writing an ambitious non-fiction book. I called my agent and asked him what he thought. He told me that truth has a way of spinning away from you, out of control. If I really thought I needed to write this book, then I should. But he warned me to be prepared to lose years of my life to the project.

On some level, most novelists write fiction to create order out of chaos. When you shape a fictional story, you can tie every loose end, fit the round pegs comfortably in circular holes. In a novel the author can create a world that makes sense.

The non-fiction writer often does the opposite. He starts with the assumption that the true story he wants to tell conforms to a logical narrative. Instead he discovers that there are always motivations that are incomprehensible. That people act irrationally. That memories are imperfect. The non-fiction writer uncovers the chaos hidden beneath the orderly surface.

I wrote another novel instead.

THIRTEEN

I remember the first time I realized that something was seriously misfiring inside Dad's brain. This was a few years ago when the networks led every hour with news of Somali pirates taking American hostages at sea. I was visiting my parents in their condo in Indiana and we were having a perfectly normal discussion, maybe about baseball. Suddenly my dad said he wanted to tell me something in private. He took me into his office, where my mother couldn't hear, and he said, "Kev, I've been talking to Captain Cornwall, and we think we have a plan to get these pirates." He had this excited look on his face, like the one he would get when he was describing a good prank. "First, we're going to drop depth charges," he said. "As a distraction."

I was confused. I said, "Are you talking about the commander of your ship? When you were in the Navy?" He said he was. I said, "That was more than fifty years ago. Captain Cornwall's been dead for decades."

In an instant he snapped out of it. "Oh yeah. Right." He laughed. "I don't know what that was about. Sorry." We went to lunch and everything was fine again.

But I was scared. And I know he was, too. My father's father had Alzheimer's. I remember a time when my

A DRIVE INTO THE GAP

cousin and I were playing at Grandpa's house—we were about six or seven—and Grandpa thought he was back on the farm where he grew up and he was trying to explain to us how to milk cows that he insisted were just outside the window. My cousin and I couldn't stop laughing. I mean really laughing. And my grandfather loved to laugh and so he started laughing too, and we were all rocking on the floor laughing uncontrollably, like little kids because my cousin and I *were* kids and my grandfather believed he was a kid once again, and I remember my grandmother coming in from the kitchen where she had been baking and I looked up at her from the floor, all of us laughing so hard we couldn't breathe, the kind of joyfully unhinged laughter most adults seem incapable of, and she had the saddest look—so full of grief and fear—that I have ever seen on another person's face.

FOURTEEN

Last year, after my dad moved into a home for patients with dementia, my sister, Ann, and I started going through his papers. He has a lot of them. Filing cabinets full. Some of these were his notes, stories from his life that he had jotted down for us. There were articles that he found interesting. A record of every fish he caught between 1980 and 1995, complete with weather conditions, the type of lure, and the section of Otsego Lake where he hooked them. We also found a few artifacts, like the typed statement he made Tony Bartirome sign, testifying with certainty that Dad's Adirondack bat was the one Clemente got his 3,000th hit with. I had heard about this document, but I'd never actually seen it.

There was also a related paper, and I'd never seen this one either. It was a memo from 1996 written by my dad to Peter Clark, the Baseball Hall of Fame registrar, the person in charge of keeping track of the exhibits.

Apparently Dad wrote it to answer a challenge to the authenticity of the Clemente bat—the Louisville Slugger—on display at the Hall. As the person who acquired the artifact, my father described how he had received the bat from Clemente himself on September

A DRIVE INTO THE GAP

30, 1972. He also repeated Tony Bartirome's claim that the Adirondack bat in Dad's possession was the true 3,000th-hit bat. But of course, my father and others had looked into this and found it untrue. Dad wrote:

> To the best of my knowledge, the bat Clemente gave me on September 30, 1972, was, in fact, the bat that I requested from him—the one he used for his 3,000th hit.

This memo was a response to a claim by a man named Les Banos, who said Clemente gave *him* the real 3,000th-hit bat on that day in 1972.

The name caused me to jump. I know Les Banos. Or I did.

Les Banos was the Pirates' team photographer in the 1970s. He was a friend of my father, and he was also a close friend of Roberto. Les was another of the many eccentrics and characters populating the Pirates' clubhouse back then. He was Hungarian, and when the Nazis occupied Hungary Les had been conscripted into the SS, but he worked as a spy for the Allies, helping an untold number of Jews escape to freedom. Les also claimed that Clemente had asked him to fly with him to Nicaragua to document relief efforts. Les said he would but had to cancel because, on December 23, 1972, the Steelers' Franco Harris made an improbable, shoestring catch of a deflected pass and scored with five seconds left to beat the Oakland Raiders and advance to the AFC Championship. That game would be played on December 31, the day of Clemente's cursed flight. Since Les was also the Steelers' team photographer, he had to stay and work.

Les always claimed that if not for the Immaculate Reception, as it's known in NFL lore, he would have died with Roberto on that chartered plane.

My own relationship with Les Banos is simple. He took more pictures of me than my parents did. As a kid I was always hanging around Three Rivers Stadium and I spent six weeks at spring training in Bradenton each year, even enrolling in a Florida school for the duration. Behind my basement bar there's an inscribed picture of kid me with catcher Manny Sanguillen (*Bueno Suerte, tu amigo...*), and another glossy 8×10 of me and my mom in our usual seats at Three Rivers. For years the background of my Twitter home page has been a photo of five-year-old me with Pirates outfielder Al Oliver, snapped by Les Banos in the spring of 1973 or so.

Wait a minute, I said. *There's another story about yet another Clemente 3,000th-hit bat? And Les Banos claims he has it?*

Reading this document I realized how incurious I had been about this story over the years. I knew my dad didn't believe Tony's version because he still had that Adirondack bat. If Dad thought it was the real 3,000th-hit bat, he would have turned it over to the Hall of Fame. It certainly wouldn't have been hanging unprotected in my old bedroom, or his new office.

But I realized that I didn't really know why he didn't believe it. And I didn't know how Tony could be so certain of his story that he'd sign his name to the bottom of it. Why didn't I ever look into this more closely?

I sat and wondered for a minute which result I had been more afraid of. If I investigated and Tony's story turned out to be true, there would be no financial windfall—obviously, my family would donate the bat to the Hall of Fame. But there would be consequences. It would be embarrassing for my father. And, to be honest, I didn't want to give it up. I really loved that bat. Until I was married it was my longest-serving roommate.

A DRIVE INTO THE GAP

And what would happen if I found out it definitely *wasn't* true? Then I'd lose a great story that I had been telling close friends for two decades.

Eighty years ago, physicist Erwin Schrödinger suggested a thought experiment in which a cat sealed in a box might be considered both alive and dead at the same time. I realize now that I wanted this bat of my father's to be the same way. If I never found out the truth it could simultaneously *be and not be* the bat Clemente got his 3,000th hit with.

For me, this was *Schrödinger's Bat*.

Forty years on I knew I finally wanted to get to the source of this tale once and for all. I wanted to open that box and discover the real journey taken by Roberto's Adirondack bat from his hands to my childhood bedroom.

And it would require something my novels often didn't.

Research.

FIFTEEN

My father couldn't answer my questions anymore. And I wasn't sure he ever knew all the answers anyway.

I called a friend of mine from high school who now works at the Baseball Hall of Fame. I asked him if they had a good photo of Clemente at the plate right before his 3,000th hit. In fifteen minutes I had it on my laptop.

I could see the ball, low and outside, just about to cross the plate. I could see Clemente's famous long swing as he stretches to reach it. The label on the bat was clearly visible. I could see the completed oval and the diagonal type—POWERIZED—right above it. A Louisville Slugger, not an Adirondack. There was no doubt.

Next, I called Tony Bartirome.

Tony is retired and lives in Florida, not far from the Pirates' spring training facility. He goes to see the workouts but never the games.

He asked about my dad. "Everyone loved your dad," Tony said. "Players, sports writers, staff. Everyone."

We reminisced a little. Tony recounted some of the jokes he used to pull on the Pirates' team physician, Dr. Finegold. One year there was a life-sized plaster statue

A DRIVE INTO THE GAP

of Clemente in the spring training clubhouse. Tony laid it on one of the training tables and unscrewed the light bulbs so it was dark. Then he sent someone to tell Doc Finegold that Clemente had passed out. The doctor rushed in the room and tried unsuccessfully to take the statue's pulse for several minutes while Tony roared in the next room.

That statue is in the Hall of Fame, too.

Finally I asked Tony about the bat. I think I expected him to tell me a tale that was full of qualifiers. *I think.* Or *I'm pretty sure. What it looked like to me.* Maybe I even expected him to tell me that it was all a practical joke after all, one of those long con kinds that my dad liked best.

Instead his story was absolutely convincing.

As he had explained to my dad, in the early innings of the game against the Mets on September 30, 1972, Clemente approached Tony in the dugout and told him and John Hallahan, the longtime equipment manager more commonly known as Hully (*HOO-lee*), that his usual bat, a Louisville Slugger (model U1), didn't feel right. Roberto really wanted to get it over with, wanted to take that rest before the playoffs, and he wasn't sure the Louisville Slugger had number 3,000 in it. He wanted to change bats.

This wasn't unprecedented, and when it happened, when for whatever reason the Louisville Slugger *didn't feel right*, Roberto would often switch to an Adirondack bat. This was slightly problematic because Clemente was under contract to use Louisville Sluggers exclusively. But the parent company, Hillerich & Bradsby, understood there would be times when one of their players wanted to experiment with a different bat. Sometimes a player would break one and grab a teammate's stick. Sometimes he wanted to try something new to snap out of a slump. Ballplayers are notoriously superstitious and sometimes their everyday bats, like Clemente's on this day, just don't feel like they have any hits in them.

And frankly, beyond free bats and the occasional perk (like golf clubs) very little cash was exchanged in these agreements. Over the course of his entire career a star like Clemente might have received $50 for a signature bat contract.

Winning was always the priority, and switching bats for a game was no big deal.

This day, however, with Clemente sitting on 2,999 hits, it was a very big deal. If he made 3,000, footage of that momentous swing would be played on newscasts all over the country. His photo would be in every paper.

There was also a rumor that Hillerich & Bradsby had offered Clemente a cash bonus for using a Louisville Slugger to get number 3,000. Almost everyone I talked to from the 1972 Pirates clubhouse knew some version of this story. One person told me he'd heard that Clemente would receive $3,000 in gold coins just for sticking with his regular bat.

Forty years on, Hillerich & Bradsby couldn't confirm the bonus rumor, but a spokesperson said it was possible that some sort of cash offer might have been on the table for an event as historic as this one.

Nevertheless, according to Tony, Clemente was convinced that his best chance of getting that hit was with an Adirondack bat.

Sometime in August, Roberto had received a shipment of Adirondacks. Bill Steele, who is still at the company, remembers the order Roberto placed in 1972. He ordered a box of bats—model 129—very similar to the model U1 Louisville Slugger he preferred. Because Clemente had no official relationship with Adirondack

A DRIVE INTO THE GAP

the barrel didn't carry his signature, just the name R CLEMENTE in block letters.

The other difference, of course, was the stripe around the middle, which would be visible to anyone in the stands or watching on TV. There in the dugout Roberto asked Tony to do something about that stripe.

Tony had a scalpel in his pocket that he used to cut athletic tape. He pulled it out and began scraping the stripe off the bat. At some point Tony was called away to attend to a player with a pulled hamstring or something, and so Tony handed the scalpel to Pirates pitcher Bob Moose and asked him to finish.

Roberto got his hit in the fourth, a double to left-center off Jon Matlack. With all eyes and camera lenses focused on second base as Clemente tipped his helmet to the crowd, Tony was thinking to himself, *I have to get that bat. I need to hide it.*

As he intercepted the batboy on his way back to the dugout, Tony was completely focused on the Adirondack in the kid's hands. "I need to take this," he said, and he ran it back to the clubhouse and hid it away in a locker.

Later that evening, after the media and most of the players had left, Tony took the bat to Roberto. "You should have this," he said. "I don't want it," Roberto told him. "You keep it." Tony said he didn't know what he'd do with it, but Roberto wouldn't accept it, so Tony locked it back up. And that's where it stayed, Tony said, for four years, until he gave the bat to Joe Brown as a retirement present. He told the story to Joe, but he didn't think Joe believed him.

Indeed, when Joe gave the bat to my father he never mentioned the story that came with it.

Tony didn't see it again for twenty years, when he stumbled across it in my old bedroom.

"But that can't be the bat he used," I told Tony when he was done. "I'm looking at a photo of his 3,000th hit that I got from the Hall of Fame. It's clearly a Louisville Slugger in his hands, not an Adirondack."

"I don't care," Tony said. "I remember everything about that day."

And I believed he was telling me the truth about what he saw. I no longer thought this story was a prank. But I was almost certainly looking at the same photo used by my dad and others at the Hall to dismiss the story back in 1993. Was it possible that Tony was right and the *photo* was wrong? Could this be a picture of a *different at bat*?

I checked the name of photographer, although I was pretty sure I knew who it was.

Les Banos.

I tried to think this all the way through. Les thought that he, and not the Hall of Fame, had the bat Roberto was swinging in one of the most famous photos Les ever snapped. According to my dad's memo, Les claimed that Roberto gave the bat to Les's son. Why would Clemente tell two different people—my dad and Les—that he was giving them each the same bat?

I needed to speak with Les. But I hadn't seen him since I was in the fifth grade. He must be more than eighty years old now.

I Googled his name and one of the first results was Les's obituary in the *Pittsburgh Post-Gazette*.

According to the time stamp on the article it had been posted seven hours ago.

Les had passed away in Pittsburgh just five days before.

SIXTEEN

I'm talking with Tom Briercheck, the Pirates' batboy from 1972 to 1976. Tom has his own bat story.

There was an old piece of lumber in the Pirates' clubhouse. Very old. It looked more like a club Fred Flintstone would carry, Tom tells me. It had initials carved in it—JPW. At first Tom thought that maybe it belonged to Paul Waner, a Pittsburgh star from the 1930s. But Hully, who had been working in the Pirates' clubhouse since he was the batboy in 1941, told a different story.

Johannes Peter Wagner, known better as Honus, played for the Pirates from 1897 to 1917. He was one of the greatest baseball players ever, one of the first five inductees into the Baseball Hall of Fame. He was also the first player ever to sign a contract to put his signature on a Louisville Slugger.

Later in life he was a coach for the Pirates, and Hully remembered Wagner carrying this bat—one of his very early bats from before his Louisville Slugger days—up and down the field as he coached. Tony Bartirome was an infielder for the Pirates when Wagner was coaching and he remembered the club, too.

Long after Honus was gone, Hully used to keep it in his equipment room, away from clubhouse mischief.

One day Richie Hebner decided to take Wagner's ancient bat for a tryout. He brought it out to batting practice and cracked it. Hully was furious. He fumed that this bat, this time-traveling totem from another era, was worthless now and he stuffed it into the garbage. Tom Briercheck rescued it and took it home and threw it under his parents' stairs. Then he forgot about it until just a couple years ago when he was cleaning some old stuff out of his father's house.

Tom confirms every part of Tony's story about the day of Clemente's final hit. He watched Tony scratch the stripe off the bat in the dugout. He remembers Tony snatching the Adirondack from his hands after the hit. I tell him I can see the Louisville Slugger label in the photo, but Tom is so sure he also wonders if the picture might really be of a different at bat. I tell him I've found a second photo of the swing, taken from a slightly different angle by a different photographer (probably from a wire service), and everything matches up—the details in the background, fans in the stands. And the Louisville Slugger in Roberto's hands.

"I don't know," Tom says. "I've been telling people for forty years that Clemente used an Adirondack bat to hit 3,000. I even said it to the guy who runs the Clemente Museum here in Pittsburgh and he told me I was crazy."

We talk about the small number of people who even knew the story. Most of them are dead now. Roberto, of course. Hully. Bob Moose, the pitcher who finished scraping off the stripe, died in a car accident before he was thirty. Joe Brown passed away two years ago. Tom jokes that there must be a curse.

Baseball voodoo or not, two people who were right there in the dugout are absolutely sure Clemente used

A DRIVE INTO THE GAP

the Adirondack to get the hit. But the thing they're so certain of can't be true.

There are clips of Clemente's 3,000th on the Internet, but to learn anything about the bat he used I need more footage and higher resolution. Maybe if I could track down the television broadcast from that day I could figure it out. Surely they would have had cameras trained on Roberto all afternoon in anticipation of the big hit.

I call a college buddy who now works at Major League Baseball in New York. He tells me I'd probably have better luck with someone in Pittsburgh. I call Jim Trdinich, the Pirates' media relations director and my old boss. They don't have it. I call Rob King, a Pittsburgh sportscaster who was a year or two ahead of me at Cooperstown High School. Rob says he'll look into it, but that a lot of Pittsburgh's archival sports footage was destroyed in a fire a few years back.

As Tom Briercheck had done before, Jim and Rob both mention the Clemente Museum.

I look up the number and I ask for Duane Rieder, a commercial photographer who founded the place. Duane recognizes my last name and gets right on the phone. We talk about Les Banos, who had been a good friend of Duane. I start to tell him the story of my dad's bat, but he's already heard it.

"You mean the Bartirome bat?"

I'm surprised. I hadn't even mentioned Tony's name.

"Do you really have it?" Duane sounds like he doesn't believe me.

"My parents do," I say.

"No way," he says. I think Duane must have thought the story was some kind of myth. "You know it's not the bat Roberto got the hit with."

"I know," I say. "But I'm trying to find out what really happened that day. How could Tony and Tom be so sure of something that can't be true? Why did Les Banos think he ended up with the real bat?" I ask Duane if he has more photos of Clemente in the on-deck circle or the dugout. Or if he knows where I might find additional news footage or a telecast of the game.

"I have something better than that," Duane says.

And he tells me another totally improbable story.

A few years ago a Clemente fan named Lou Schmitt walked into the museum with several spools of Super 8 home movies that hadn't been seen by anyone in forty years. He needed help transferring them to DVD. And the tale of how he made the film was as incredible as the footage itself.

The phone is shaking in my hand as Duane retells it. I had been wishing for something, for something very specific, something that didn't exist, that couldn't exist, and now Duane was telling me that it *did exist* and he had it. I suddenly felt like I could will things into being with my mind.

"How can I see this film, Duane?" I ask.

"When can you come to Pittsburgh?" he says.

SEVENTEEN

Two years after Roberto's death, I attended a dinner honoring him. Many eulogized him, remembering his many accomplishments during the sixteen years he played with the Pirates.

Then Dan Galbreath, president of the Pirates, stood up. "I'd like to share with you," he said, "a letter I received from Roberto several weeks before he died."

It was a two-page letter and Mr. Galbreath read excerpts from it: "Thanks for the privilege of playing for the Pirates. I couldn't ask for better teammates and the Pirate fans are the greatest in baseball. Everyone has been so kind to Vera and the children. Whenever you think I can no longer contribute to the team's success, I will retire. I thank you and the Pirate organization for being so good to me and my family."

The last sentence of the letter read: "I promise I will never play for any other team."

EIGHTEEN

"I don't know if I'd still have the guts today to do what I did that afternoon. But I loved watching Clemente. I loved watching anything he would do."

I'm on the phone with Lou Schmitt, who retired to Dallas a few years ago after a successful career in the consulting business. In 1972, he was a twenty-six-year-old father living just north of Pittsburgh, and a huge Roberto Clemente fan. He was watching from the right-field stands on the Friday night when Roberto had number 3,000 snatched away by the official scorer. The next day he was sure the game would be sold out, but he knew he had to be there. He knew he had to be at the game when his lifelong hero became one of the immortals.

So he started to make a plan that would bring him just an arm's length from history.

He dressed his two sons, Dan and Boomer, in Pirates uniforms with Willie Stargell's number 8 and Clemente's number 21 on their backs. Then he and his boys and his wife Carol drove to Three Rivers Stadium early in the day and walked up to the players' entrance. Lou had dressed himself up in a suit and he carried with him a

A DRIVE INTO THE GAP

Nikon Super 8 movie camera with a tripod. He told the guard that his sons had won a contest to be honorary batboys for the day.

The guard said he didn't know anything about it. Lou had anticipated this reaction, of course, because he had made it all up. He'd even prepared a response. Before he left home, he'd opened the Pirates' yearbook, turned to the staff page, and looked up the name of the Pirates' executive in charge of public relations.

"Bill Guilfoile invited us," Lou told the guard.

In that case, the guard said, it should be no problem. "Bill is probably having lunch upstairs in the Allegheny Club about now. I'll call up there, get Bill on the phone, and we'll straighten this all out."

When the guard got my father on the phone, Dad said he didn't know anything about it, either. Now Lou figured he was screwed.

"Let me talk to him," Lou said, and the guard handed him the phone.

Lou pretty much confessed his scam to my dad. But he made his case as best he could. He said, "Mr. Guilfoile, my name is Lou Schmitt and my kids are here, and I'm a big Roberto fan and I would love to share this day with them. If you could get us on the field for a few minutes before the game, I'd really appreciate it."

My father said he couldn't do it. There were a lot of people who wanted to be on the field that day, including many VIPs and assorted dignitaries. In fact the governor-elect of Puerto Rico was down there already. "But I'll tell you what," my dad told Lou. "Call me in the spring. We'll arrange for your sons to be honorary batboys at a game next season. They can come down on the field and meet Roberto and the other players next year, and it will all be official."

Lou thought it was a kind offer, but he also knew he needed to get in the ballpark *today*, not next spring. He couldn't give up. He couldn't go home.

But he knew what he *could* do.

Into the phone he said, "Mr. Guilfoile, thank you so much! I can't tell you how much the boys and I appreciate that!"

And then he hung up.

"What did Bill say?" the guard asked.

Lou smiled. "He said we can go on the field!"

NINETEEN

Shortly after the 1972 season, Roberto hosted a dinner in Puerto Rico honoring Pirates broadcaster Bob Prince. It was Clemente's way of showing his appreciation for Bob's many kindnesses to him over the years. My wife Loretta and I, and Bernadette and Nellie King (Bob's broadcast partner) had also been invited, along with Betty and Bob Prince, as Roberto's guests. During the dinner Roberto expressed his thanks to Bob and told him he had a special gift for him. He then presented Prince with a treasure only Clemente could give— a treasure only Roberto WOULD give: The silver bat awarded to him for winning the batting championship in 1961. It was a truly magnanimous gesture and one that left Bob Prince speechless for the first time in his life.

TWENTY

"Sorry about the smell. The grapes arrived over the weekend and we're doing the crush downstairs."

I am in the Clemente Museum, in the Lawrenceville section of Pittsburgh. It's an amazing space, a former firehouse where Lou Gehrig once slept while visiting a firefighter pal, with a photographer's studio on the top floor, a beautiful museum dedicated to Roberto on the first floor, and, believe it or not, a fully equipped winery in the basement.

Duane founded the museum several years ago. He'd been working on a calendar for the Pirates and flew to San Juan to photograph some items at Vera Clemente's home. Over time, Vera and Duane agreed that many of these items, not just photos and contracts, but uniforms and gold gloves and World Series rings, should be on display in Pittsburgh where Clemente's most devoted fans could see them. Duane started a foundation with Vera on the board and the museum was born.

Duane's first love is photography and the museum has dozens of stunning photos of Clemente, as well as an enormous archive of negatives—many donated by Les Banos—that Duane hasn't had time to completely

A DRIVE INTO THE GAP

sort. Les had been a family friend of the Clementes and in addition to the famous action shots, he took many personal photos of the family, in private moments away from the field.

One black-and-white photo, taken by a Pittsburgh newspaper photographer, dominates a wall of the main gallery. Clemente is posed against the sky. A pair of feathery, symmetrical clouds seem to sprout from his back like an angel's wings.

"Not Photoshopped," Duane says.

But I'm really here to see Lou Schmitt's movie. And the story of this film takes me back, once again, to September 30, 1972.

After Lou hung up with my dad, the guard led the Schmitt family right into the dugout and left them alone with their Super 8 camera.

Lou began to film. And as I watch his movie on a big Apple computer screen, I actually have chills.

The stands behind home plate are starting to fill in. Through Lou's lens we see Bob Prince talking with one of the Pirates' assistant coaches. We see future Hall of Famer Bill Mazeroski, who was about to retire, walking around with a plaque of some sort. Dan and Boomer Schmitt are watching from a distance. Les Banos makes an appearance in his black-and-gold Pirates jacket, camera in hand. Two other young boys are there, also in uniforms—probably the *actual* honorary batboys that day. There's an official-looking man in an official-looking suit. Possibly the governor of Puerto Rico.

Suddenly Clemente appears, posing for photos and receiving his own plaques and accolades. At first Carol

Schmitt keeps her boys out of his way, but Roberto finds them soon enough. He gives them each a finger to shake and then he kneels and signs their gloves with a pen. He could leave at that point, but he doesn't. He leans closer to talk with each of them. The boys are shy. He puts his arm around their shoulders. He asks them questions. He laughs at their answers.

Carol glances at Lou. *Can you believe this? Are you getting this?*

Cut to the first inning. Lou is in the photographers' well now, right next to the Pirates' dugout. Incredibly, no one has told him to leave. Roberto is in the on-deck circle, with teenage batboy Tom Briercheck standing right behind him. The game has started but Schmitt is interested only in Clemente.

Lou Schmitt is my hero.

Roberto has two bats with him. You can't make out the labels but one of them clearly has the Adirondack stripe around the middle. When it's his turn, he lets the Adirondack fall to his feet and takes a Louisville Slugger to the plate.

On the way he passes Briercheck, who is headed back to the dugout with a pair of bats, presumably ones belonging to center fielder Rennie Stennett, who had just grounded into a double play.

The crowd is thin in the upper decks but they're packed in behind home. The fans greet Roberto with a standing ovation. He lets the bat swing easily in front of him as he steps to the batter's box.

Settled in, Clemente takes two balls and a strike, then he swings, awkwardly, at Jon Matlack's fourth pitch. He takes a stab at strike three, but he has no chance—his body corkscrews 270 degrees past the ball. As the Mets jog in from the field, Clemente drops both helmet and Louisville Slugger at home plate.

A DRIVE INTO THE GAP

Walking back to the dugout, Roberto looks exactly like a guy who hadn't slept all night.

The next time we see Clemente with a helmet on, in the on-deck circle in the third inning, he has two bats once again.

There's no sign of a stripe on either of them.

Clemente doesn't bat that inning. Stennett makes the third out while Roberto's on deck.

I know from talking to Lou Schmitt that it's around this time that Les Banos asks Lou for his press credentials, and when he can't produce them Les tells Lou to leave the field. Lou is panicked. He's gotten this far. He can't miss the hit.

Just then a cameraman for WTAE, Pittsburgh's ABC affiliate, leaves the photo area and climbs up into the stands behind first base. Lou follows him and finds an empty seat. Like Richie Hebner, he can't believe there are so many of them.

When Lou turns the camera back on he's filming from a slightly higher vantage point, over the dugout. Clemente is leading off the fourth inning. Willie Stargell, who bats right after Clemente, is already stretching in the on-deck circle. Roberto has two bats in his hands, but then he stops and goes back in the dugout. When he reemerges he has three bats. None of them has a stripe. He leans over next to Stargell and asks Willie something.

Stargell grips the bats one at a time and wiggles them, getting a feel for each. Then he hands Clemente one of the bats. It's a bit of a shell game, but I think Stargell finally decides on the third one, the one Roberto went back into the dugout to get at the last minute. Clemente lets the other two bats fall to the ground and he steps up to the plate.

Two pitches later, he's circling first on his way to 3,000.

I step through this home movie like it's the Zapruder film. After about an hour Duane asks me if I've figured it out. I tell him, I think so.

Clemente goes out in the first with his usual Louisville Slugger and my dad's Adirondack. He strikes out with the Louisville Slugger.

We don't see it on the film, but we can assume it's sometime in the bottom of the second inning, after the Pirates come in from the field, when Roberto tells Tony to make the Adirondack stripe disappear because he wants to use that bat the next time up. In the third inning he goes out with the Louisville Slugger, plus the scraped-off Adirondack. He doesn't hit, though. In the fourth inning he walks out with those two bats again, then he goes back for a second Louisville Slugger. Maybe he was having second thoughts about using an Adirondack for such an important at bat.

I had checked with Hillerich & Bradsby and discovered that Clemente ordered three different weights of bats from them that year—the 36-ounce bat he preferred, plus a smaller number of 37- and 38-ounce bats. My guess is that in the fourth inning, Roberto went out to the on-deck circle with a bat of every weight: He had the 36-ounce Louisville Slugger that he struck out with in the first, the 37-ounce Adirondack with the stripe missing, and a 38-ounce Louisville Slugger that he retrieved from the bat rack at the last minute. I suspect Stargell chose the 38-ouncer, and there's circumstantial evidence to back me up on that. According to David Maraniss's 2006 biography *Clemente*, Roberto met with his Louisville Slugger rep in Cincinnati just a few days later and talked about upping his order of 38-ounce bats for 1973.

So Clemente drops the Adirondack in the on-deck circle and Tom Briercheck picks it up while Clemente hits. Tom holds on to it, as he usually does, in case

A DRIVE INTO THE GAP

Roberto breaks his bat and needs another quickly. After Clemente gets the hit, Tom runs out to home plate and picks up the Louisville Slugger Roberto used. Then he heads back to the dugout with both bats in his hands.

Meanwhile, Tony Bartirome, who never saw the back and forth between Clemente and Stargell, assumes Roberto used the Adirondack as he said he would. Tony takes that bat from Briercheck and hides it away. It happened exactly the way Tony saw it. He was just missing one piece of information. After consulting with Stargell, Roberto changed his mind at the last minute. He used a different bat. A Louisville Slugger.

I call Tom Briercheck and ask him if my theory is possible. "I always thought he used the Adirondack," Tom says. "But if you're sure from the photos that he used a Louisville Slugger, then that's probably exactly what happened."

Forty years after Roberto's 3,000th hit, and almost twenty years after Tony Bartirome told my dad a completely convincing but impossible story, the mystery was finally solved.

I go over the Schmitt film one more time with Duane. "So after the game, my dad goes down to the clubhouse, asks Roberto for the bat, and he gives Dad the Louisville Slugger he got the hit with."

"No," Duane says.

"What do you mean?" I say.

He says, "The Hall of Fame definitely has the wrong bat."

I ask Duane what he's talking about.

"Watch the end of the film," he tells me.

TWENTY-ONE

About six months before my father went into the memory center where he now lives, I went to stay with him for a few days. My mother was going to visit relatives in New York and while my dad's condition wasn't bad enough for a nursing home yet, no one thought he could get by on his own, even for a weekend.

We had a good time. We ate at restaurants. Watched basketball. Went for walks. During the day, he was pretty good, although he had a lot of inertia. He wouldn't do anything unless I suggested it, but when I did, he would tackle it with his usual enthusiasm.

"Are you hungry?" I'd ask, and he'd reply, "Boy, am I!" but I got the feeling he wouldn't even make himself a sandwich if I wasn't there.

He would also ask me every hour where Mom was. I would tell him and he would chuckle and say, "Oh that's right! Why can't I remember?" Then he would ask again. By the second day he at least knew he was supposed to know the answer, but he had to ask anyway.

After dark, he would become very confused. The first night, a little after midnight, he knocked on my bedroom door and woke me up. The door wasn't locked but Dad

A DRIVE INTO THE GAP

didn't open it. He said, "Excuse me. Is Loretta Guilfoile there? This is her husband, Bill, and I'm a little embarrassed, but I don't know where she is."

I said, "Just a second, Dad." I got out of bed and I walked to the door and for a few seconds we just stood on either side of it, listening to each other breathe. I think I was as scared to open it as he was.

Because I had a feeling that when I did, for the first time in my life, my father wouldn't be able to recognize me.

TWENTY-TWO

Duane and I watch the rest of the movie together. Clemente comes out of the game shortly after his hit and retreats into the clubhouse to celebrate with a small entourage of his friends. Incredibly, Lou and his camera follow them right into the Pirates' locker room sanctuary.

You could never, ever do that today. Lou Schmitt has more balls than a batting practice pitcher.

Looking at this film is like staring into a crystal ball. We shouldn't be able to watch this scene from so long ago, yet we do. Vera comes down and Roberto meets her tenderly by the clubhouse door. We see Les Banos snapping photos again, as well as a number of Clemente's friends. One of them appears to be José Santiago, a former Major League pitcher, also from Puerto Rico. He is carrying a bat.

Duane pulls a photo from his files, a picture Les took right at the same time Lou Schmitt was in the clubhouse shooting his Super 8 film. Clemente is still in uniform. Santiago is wearing the same suit he's wearing in the home movie. They are holding a bat together, apparently presenting it to the lens as the bat he hit 3,000 with.

A DRIVE INTO THE GAP

"The bat in the Hall of Fame is much cleaner than this bat. It doesn't have as many ball marks."

I had seen the bat in the Hall hundreds of times as a kid. I'd recently seen a photo of it. That bat is pretty clean, and the bat in this photo looks like it had been used in a few games. The handle looks like it might have more pine tar than the Hall's bat. But this photo of Clemente and Santiago was taken almost forty years ago in a dark clubhouse. Could I say for sure that the bat in this photo is different than the bat in the Hall of Fame? Duane seems certain, but I'm not.

"If the real bat's not in the Hall, where is it?" I ask.

Duane says he isn't sure. Les Banos claimed that Clemente gave the bat to Les's son, but Duane doesn't think Les ever had it either. He tells me of a rumor that a family out East claims to have it. They were close to the Clementes and they say Roberto gave the real one to them that day.

"Wait," I say. "So it's possible Roberto told at least *three different people*, including my dad, that he was giving them the bat he got his 3,000th hit with?"

"Looks that way," Duane says.

TWENTY-THREE

Back home in Chicago the next day, I call Ted Spencer in Cooperstown. Ted's retired now, but he was curator of the Hall of Fame for twenty-seven years and was a close colleague of my father. He knows the Hall of Fame's Clemente bat as well as anybody. I tell him what I saw in Pittsburgh. I tell him about the trio of alleged 3,000th-hit bats that might be out there.

Ted doesn't sound surprised.

"Every bat in the Hall of Fame has a story like this," he says. "Do you know how many Boston cops claim Ted Williams gave him the bat from his 500th home run?" Ted explains that back then memorabilia wasn't the business it is today. These artifacts weren't worth hundreds of thousands of dollars. Players would frequently tell their friends—sometimes multiple friends—that they were giving them this bat or that ball as a special gift. It made them happy. To Ted Williams, having a bunch of cops who owed him a favor was probably more valuable than any old bat.

One of the impressive things about the Clemente bat in the Hall, Ted says, is that its provenance is rock solid. Clemente gave it to my dad specifically for the purpose

A DRIVE INTO THE GAP

of sending it to the Baseball Hall of Fame. My father was close to Clemente, and Clemente gave him the bat to preserve it for posterity. "No one who knows your father would ever question his integrity," Ted says.

I ask him about the picture Clemente took with José Santiago. Personally I can't say for sure, but I can see how someone, like Duane Rieder, might look at that photo and say the bat looks dirtier than the one in the Hall.

Ted reminds me of the iconic photo of Bobby Thomson kissing his bat in the clubhouse after he hit the home run giving the New York Giants the National League pennant in 1951. If you know anything about baseball history you know the famous Russ Hodges call of that hit: "The Giants win the pennant! The Giants win the pennant! The Giants win the pennant!"

"The bat in that Thomson photo isn't the real bat," Ted says. Both Bobby Thomson and Giants pitcher Hal Schumacher confirmed that the actual bat wasn't nearby when the photographer was ready to take the picture. They just grabbed any old bat, because it was convenient. But everybody who looks at that photo assumes it was the bat that launched The Shot Heard Round the World.

With memorabilia, provenance is almost everything. In a way, the 3,000th-hit bat didn't become the 3,000th-hit bat when Clemente smacked that double into the gap. It became the 3,000th-hit bat when Roberto gave it to the Hall of Fame and said, "This is the bat I did it with."

The bat isn't the valuable thing. It's just a bat like every other. It's the *story* that's valuable. And it was Clemente himself who attached the story of his 3,000th hit to that Louisville Slugger in the Hall of Fame.

Whether or not he used it to get the hit, Roberto cast a spell on that bat when he handed it to my dad. It would take more than an old photo to undo that magic.

TWENTY-FOUR

I'm watching the Schmitt movie again. But I'm no longer interested in a frame-by-frame dissection of Roberto's movements in the on-deck circle. Now I'm watching Roberto before the game, talking to Dan and Boomer, Lou Schmitt's kids.

This was one of the biggest, most stressful days of Roberto's life. He had to know that he'd be remembered for his 3,000th hit as much as anything he did in his career. We know he hadn't slept the night before. We know he was torturing himself about small details like which bat he should use. He had every reason to be stressed out. Cranky.

But here he is just minutes before the game, laughing with a stranger's kids, a couple of kids who shouldn't even have been there. And he's giving them a lot more time than he needs just to humor them. After he said hello and signed their gloves he could have walked away and it would have been one of the best days in these boys' lives. But he doesn't leave. He doesn't look like he has anyplace else to be.

When you're as talented and famous as Barry Bonds or Roberto Clemente, too much is going to be expected

A DRIVE INTO THE GAP

of you. The demands on you will never end. And you can react to those demands in a number of different ways. Barry Bonds decided that he would just never give anybody anything, because he knew if he gave them one thing today they would ask for three things tomorrow. And he was probably right about that, as wrong as it must have been for his soul.

Roberto decided to do the opposite. If you asked him for one thing, he gave you four. He worked hard to become one of the best who ever played the game, and then he gave away the trophies that proved it.

He gave as much as he could. He gave more than he could.

On the day of one of his biggest triumphs he might have told three different friends he was giving them the same historic baseball bat.

He never stopped giving.

He gave right up until the day that giving literally killed him.

TWENTY-FIVE

The pictures on the walls of my dad's room don't represent a complete retrospective of his life, but they hit on a lot of the highlights.

There's a photo of Captain Cornwall, and one of their ship, the USS *Snyder*. There's a photo of Mantle and one of Clemente. A photo of Dad shaking hands with Ronald Reagan at a White House dinner honoring the Baseball Hall of Fame. There's a large painting of an imaginary gathering of all the Pirates greats, from Honus Wagner to Willie Stargell. On his desk there's a photo of my mom, and pictures of their grandchildren.

We're on the couch watching Lou Schmitt's movie on my laptop. I tell Dad how Lou used his name to sneak into the ballpark that day. Dad doesn't remember his phone conversation with Lou, nor does he understand the forehead-slapping, *Back to the Future*, time-traveling significance of it all—that Dad played an unwitting but critical role in the making of an amazing film that, four decades later, we would use to discover the true history of his bat. But he thinks the story's really funny.

Watching the video he tears up a few times. I can't tell if it's out of nostalgia or because his memories of that

A DRIVE INTO THE GAP

day have turned into shadows. "There were some good players on that team," he says. Four or five times he says, unprompted, "We had some good days, didn't we?"

I ask him if he remembers going down to the clubhouse to get Roberto's bat after the game. He does. "Were there a lot of reporters?" I ask.

"Not too many," he says. "Some."

"Did Roberto have the bat right there with him? At his locker?"

"No," Dad says. "He had to go and get it, as I recall." He sounds a little surprised even as he says it. But he doesn't remember much else.

We talk about other things. Somehow my mother gets on the subject of redheads, and how red-headedness is a recessive gene. "My father was a redhead, and my grandfather, too," Mom says to me. "But your father didn't have any redheads in his family so none of you kids have it."

Dad, who's been quiet for a while, grins and says, "I'll come through for you one of these days!" He's still funny.

My youngest son is in a chair playing Angry Birds on my phone. A few hours into our visits, my father will almost always begin to call him "Kev," mistaking my five-year-old for me. When this happens I always wonder who he thinks I am. Sometimes Dad gets very formal, shaking my hand as if we'd just met, and thanking me for coming. When it happens today, perhaps because we talked for so long about the Pirates, he apparently thinks I'm a ballplayer.

"You set such a good example for the other players," he tells me. "You were so nice and so accommodating to the fans. The other players looked up to you, and followed your example. That made my job easier. Thank you."

I tell him it was no problem.

"Your family was always so nice to everyone, too," he says. "I appreciated that."

On the way home we stop by Mom's condo to pick up a few things. I wander into my dad's old office and pull Clemente's Adirondack off the wall. It's enormous—probably four inches longer than the Mickey Mantle Louisville Slugger next to it.

Mom shows me a picture of her and my dad when he was in the Navy and they were still dating. They're standing with my grandmother in front of Yankee Stadium, where just a few years later Dad will go to work each day. I think of all the stuff that happened between that picture and now that he can no longer remember. I think about how smart he was to write so much of it down. To leave a trail we can always use to find him.

We had some good days, didn't we?

ACKNOWLEDGEMENTS

Sincere thanks to everyone named in this story, as well as to Sally O'Leary, Elizabeth Meyer, P.J. Shelley, Susan McKay, Peter Clark, Fran Althiser, Milo Stewart, and Michael Mandarano.

And, of course, thank you Mom and Dad.

—kg

ABOUT THE AUTHOR

Kevin Guilfoile is the best-selling author of two acclaimed novels, *Cast of Shadows* and *The Thousand*, which have been translated into more than 20 languages. He once met Barbara Bush, who totally had him convinced that her English springer spaniel, Millie, had been trained as a bomb-sniffing dog. But that's another story.

ABOUT THE TYPE

The text of this book is set in Century Schoolbook (1918), one of 221 typefaces designed by American typography titan Morris Fuller Benton (1872-1948). Century Schoolbook is based on Benton's father Linn Boyd Benton's Century typeface, created for *Century* magazine in 1894. The younger Benton's version was created at the request of textbook publisher Ginn & Co., with the intent of improved legibility.

Century and its variants were originally published by American Type Founders. Formed by a merger of 23 foundries in 1892, ATF quickly became the dominant force in American typography until the mid-20th-century, largely thanks to the Benton's typographical and technological innovations. Century is often cited as the first true typeface "family," a concept quickly embraced by type designers, foundries, and users.

Section headers are set in Futura, the celebrated geometric sans-serif face created by German type designer Paul Renner for the Bauer Type Foundry in 1927. Informed by the Bauhaus and Futurist movements, Renner sought to simplify sans-serif type to its necessary geometric elements. Futura's popularity has rarely waned through the decades since its introduction.

ABOUT FIELD NOTES BRAND

Inspired by the vanishing subgenre of agricultural memo books, ornate pocket ledgers, and the simple, unassuming beauty of a well-crafted grocery list, the Draplin Design Company, Portland, Oregon, and Coudal Partners of Chicago, Illinois, have created the Field Notes Brand line of memo books and related products, which are available online and in retail stores around the world.

Four times each year, Field Notes releases a limited edition of themed memo books which are available individually and by subscription. *A Drive into the Gap* is the first release from Field Notes Brand Books and is being published alongside our seasonal memo books for the summer of 2012, "The Day Game Edition."

FIELD NOTES
fieldnotesbrand.com

"I'm not writing it down to remember it later, I'm writing it down to remember it now."